# Snapshots of Cramlington Life

A Remembrance Ceremony at the newly dedicated
War Memorial, Cramlington Village in the 1920s.
A poignant photograph that was printed with a
black border.

# by Brian Godfrey

*Above*: East Cramlington Methodist Church, Sunday School group, circa 1914. The building is still in use but its days as a place of worship ended many years ago.

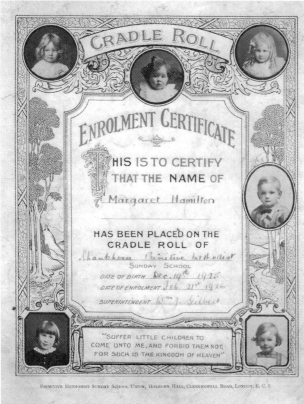

*Left*: Margaret Hamilton was born on 19th December 1925 and was enrolled into the Methodist Church two months later in February 1926. The 'Cradle Roll' signified that Margaret was entered on the church register, was recognised, accepted and baptised in the Primitive Methodist religion.

Copyright Brian Godfrey 2016

First published in 2016 by

Summerhill Books, PO Box 1210, Newcastle-upon-Tyne NE99 4AH

www.summerhillbooks.co.uk     email: summerhillbooks@yahoo.co.uk

ISBN: 978-1-911385-11-0

# Introduction

While professional portraits, views and group photographs of the past are evocative and informative, the humble snapshot appears to have been overlooked. Cramlington, like all communities, has a hidden social history which is revealed in part, through these sometimes, grainy, creased, torn and indistinct images. I hope that the images in this book and the stories behind some of them will go some way in revealing a little of Cramlington social history.

*Brian Godfrey*
*Cramlington, November 2016*

The back lane of Blue Top Row, High Pit in 1937. While neighbours look on, Max Mullen and his twin brother Gordon enjoy an outdoor bath. Max's parents had eleven children all told and were brought up within the tiny confines of a colliery house. The present Blue Top Cottages now occupy the site.

# Acknowledgements

My thanks for their contributions to this work go to: Edwina Straughan, Doreen Morton, George Purvis, Doreen Bell, Marjorie Mullen, Muriel Smith, Colin Nevins, Mike Garnham, Harry Temple, Margaret Black, Brian Coppen, John Coppen, Dennis Green, Sharon Philipson, Brian Leighton, Kathleen of the Blyth Battery, Jody Wilson, Malcolm Gibson, John Stephens, Jim and Rosemary Harland.

*This book is dedicated to*
*Kevin Wilson, 1951 - 2016*

# Snapshots of Cramlington

Cramlington House, in its final incarnation as the head office of the coal board. Built in the early 19th century by the Lawson family, it successively became the home of a family named Potter and then the residence of reigning chief engineers of Cramlington Coal Company. The house was pulled down in 1969 and the site cleared for the building of Lanercost Park.

*Left*: Martin Thompson's House just prior to its demolition in the 1970s.

*Below*: Two photos of Martin Thompson's House in the process of demolition. In the bottom right photo, in the left background, can be seen the bungalow which was to become the Lal Qila Indian restaurant. Beyond that is the gable of John the Clerk of Cramlington, formerly the Travellers Rest.

West farm in the 1970s – a typical Northumbrian stone farm building of the mid 19th century. Upstairs was a space which seemed to have been utilised as a meeting and entertainment venue as a stage had been built at one end, the walls still retained painted decoration and gas mantles had been installed around the walls. Now West Farm Court.

The derelict cottages, built in the early 19th century, that once stood on the site now occupied by H. Duckworth undertakers. At some point the furthest end cottage was converted into a shop and a window was let into its gable end wall – seen on postcards from the early 20th century. It was once occupied by Jason Ferrow, undertaker, before becoming the premises of H. Duckworth. I believe the cottages were called 'Woodbine Terrace' or 'Row'. This 1960s photo shows the Methodist Chapel standing across the road.

The photograph was taken in June of 1928 and shows Ralph, his brother Bob Turnbull and young Bob Potts. They stand holding tools of the blacksmith's trade outside of the old 'Smithy' in Cramlington Village. The row of cottages behind them were demolished some years later leaving only the 'Smithy'. It still had a working

forge well into the 1960s and was demolished in 1974, leaving only the name 'Smithy Square'. The large hoop is an iron tire for a wooden cart wheel. The gradual decline in the use of horse drawn transport heralded the end of traditional blacksmithing.

An early photograph of miners at Hartford Colliery, possibly in the early 1900s. The fierce looking chap at centre with beard sports a regulation bowler hat, indicative of an 'overman' while the others have soft caps, some of which have fold down ear flaps that tie under the chin. All wear the common dress of most working men of the time. They no doubt dressed, while not working, in a dark suit with waistcoat and a white kneckcloth, giving according to a traveller underground in 1856, 'A semi-parsonic air'. This he attributed to the spread of Methodism in the coal fields. Rather like the keelmen of the Wear and Tyne who liked to distinguish themselves through their dress, the old time miners of Northumberland did

likewise. The young pitman would wear the hair at temples in curls with the longest hair in plaits or tails tied with ribbons. His waistcoat he would call his 'Posy vest' as it was embroidered with colourful flowers. Velveteen or plush breeches were tied at the knee with ribbons, stockings and stout boots gave him a sound foundation. The whole was topped off with a round boater like hat on which long coloured ribbons were optional to the wearer. Thus regaled, our 'Bonnie Pit Laddie' would step out for some well earned fun at quoits or bowls or simply getting drunk and fighting. All of this was swept away however when the 'religion of the coalfields' made Sundays a whole lot quieter.

*Left*: Another early view of Hartford Colliery shows cauldron wagons waiting to be filled with full ones behind them.

Built by Robert Stephenson & Co, Engineers, Newcastle upon Tyne in 1889, this engine carries the No 7841 and was used to haul coal trucks from Hartford Colliery to the screens at Shankhouse.

Lamb Pit, East Cramlington, probably in the 1930s, showing the aerial cable way that carried the buckets to the slag heaps where they were emptied and returned to the screens empty.

The brick kilns at East Cramlington in 1973.

These are the remains of East Cramlington Colliery in 1973.

A goods train heading north, passes a trackside workmen's cabin and Cramlington signal box.

The shot provides a better view of the back of Station Terrace than it does of the engine – southbound.

A nice view of the Station buildings and staff houses with a southbound passenger train passing through.

An early 'Deltic' class diesel loco hauling a goods train passes beneath the original two arch bridge southbound. The arch at right allowed the siding tracks access to the engine shed. The aged miners' cottages are in the background.

A lovely shot of a northbound express; loaded wagons stand in the sidings at the left.

A 'Pacific' class loco, hauling a passenger train, steams by the Station master's house, at right. The Station master at the time was a Mr Franklin. The houses at the centre are in Nelson Village.

*Left:* A northbound goods train passes under the original Victorian cast iron footbridge. The waiting room on the right was also an original feature with reasonably comfortable seating and a fireplace.

An 'atmospheric' snap of a Pacific class loco and passenger train passing southbound through the station.

A single loco enters the station northbound, passing under the original bridge.

*Left:* A goods train passes under the New Road bridge, southbound. 'Stanley Houses' are in the background on the right.

Its is known that the airship shed at Nelson Village was used during the Second World War as a centre for constructing heavy army vehicles. The components for the vehicles were shipped in and the vehicles were put together within the vast space the shed afforded. These were usually the American Army trucks and it would be safe to assume

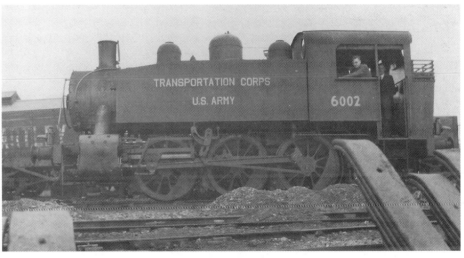

that this photo (marked Cramlington 1945) was used in connection with this process. This engine, 'S100' 0-6-OT, was one of three USA Army transport corps 'S100S' bought by the National Coal Board in 1947 as war surplus. The engines were put to work in the former Hartley Main area of Northumberland, mainly in hauling coals to the River Tyne. (In the left background is a Hartley Mains coal wagon.) Two of these engines were employed in this way until they were scrapped in 1953. The last of the trio worked at the Rising Sun Colliery at Wallsend until 1954 when it to was scrapped.

*Left:* The 'Airship Shed' at Nelson Village in the mid 1960s. This view of the 'Shed' gives an idea of how it managed to dominate not only the surrounding houses but also the skyline.

Dr Robert Forsyth at the gate of his home and surgery, No 1 Blagdon Terrace. Dr Forsyth, a much respected MD, served Cramlington and surrounding communities for many years until his death in March 1927.

Uncle Jimmy Harsant deciding whether he should try a quick reviver. The Co-op central buildings can be seen at the right in the 1960s.

Master butcher Joseph Garnham (centre) and his colleagues strike a proud pose outside Cramlington Co-op Butchery Department, Cramlington Village in the 1940s.

W.H. Endean with his 'pride and joy' at Philipson's Garage, circa 1950. The Old School buildings can be seen in the background. W.H. died in 1956, aged 86 years.

Les Armstrong Newsagents, Klondyke in the mid 1970s. The photograph shows the condition of the unmettled streets at the time. A group of young lads await the arrival of the evening newspaper editions. A job as a 'Paperboy' was much sought after and most newsagents held a waiting list.

The papers arrive and the boys help to unload the bundles from the van. Jimmy Amours shop can be seen at left, with a sign above the window, Jimmy ran a small business literally from his front room, selling sweets and odds and ends. He also sold mince pies which were heated in his oven.

This beautiful old Wolseley belonged to Harry James. It was blue and white, had leather seats and was a dream to drive. She is parked in front of Harry's shop at Klondyke. The James family also owned the drapery business next door and the hardware shop, the low building at the right. The scene has changed some what since the early 1970s snap. Chinese and Indian takeaways now occupy the shops at the left, while the 'Hut' has been replaced by a row of modern rental premises.

A regular visitor to Cramlington in the 1970s was 'Robinson Mobile Chippy'. Here is parked on the Old Road that ran by the now, Lal Qila Restaurant down through Sunnyside. A queue of eager punters await the delights of the travelling epicurean. Cramlington new shopping centre is under construction in the background.

Another snap taken in Sunnyside, probably late 1960s. The day could well be Friday when most 'vans' would be on the road until late, as this was the main shopping day. The good dames of Sunnyside are being spoilt as they have already had a visit from the grocery van. The fruit and vegetables and butchers van have now made an appearance. Would this kind of service be successful today? Given the amount of shopping that can be seen piled into trolleys at any supermarket,

travelling shops would need to be many times larger than they were. Shopping for provisions used to be done with one or two relatively small shopping bags for the week at a local branch. The vans were handy as a 'Top up'. I suppose the moral here is that the more there is on sale the more we tend to buy and that we want very much more than we actually need.

George Moor in 1982. George delivered milk every morning, usually beginning his far flung round at 1 am. This was because his customers were so widespread, not only in Cramlington but also in Hartford, Seaton Delaval, Dudley and probably even further. It was a bit of a mystery as to when he actually slept as, after his round, work on the farm occupied his day.

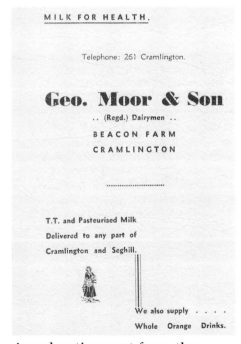

MILK FOR HEALTH,

Telephone: 261 Cramlington.

# Geo. Moor & Son

.. (Regd.) Dairymen ..

BEACON FARM
CRAMLINGTON

T.T. and Pasteurised Milk
Delivered to any part of
Cramlington and Seghill.

We also supply . . . .
Whole Orange Drinks.

An advertisement from the pages of the 'Geordie Broon of Backworth' series from the 1930s. George is the 'And Son'.

On Station Road looking towards Cramlington Village, the houses on the left are still recognisable but the building in the centre is long gone. Built originally in the early 1900s as a post office, it later became a chemist and stood empty for many years until demolished.

The building to the right were built by Cramlington Co-op as dwellings for employees – removed in the mid 1970s.

In snapping his pigeons returning to the loft, George Purvis has given us a view of the Station Cottages Gardens and a glimpse of the Station Master's house on the left. The Station car park and the Royal Mail building now occupy the site.

Old friends stop for a chat on Station Terrace in the 1970s. The terrace was built in the 1890s. It was demolished to make way for the new shopping areas a few years after this photograph was taken.

The 21st birthday celebration of William Lawson held at the Store Hall, High Pit, has spilled out on to the main road for this 1939 photograph. High Pit Club is the building top right. Try sitting in the middle of the road today but don't be surprised by the result.

*Right:* High Pit CIU Club receiving modernisation and extension in 1974. The origins of the club go back to the First World War when local men who had served in the armed forces returned to Cramlington. A large wooden hut was constructed on land directly behind Robinson's Dental Practice. Little is known about the purpose of the building, aptly named the 'Dardanelles' but there must have been an element of recuperation,

healing through the comradeship of shared experiences. Indeed, old maps record the building as a hospital. From these humble but worthy beginnings developed the club that offered more or less the same as the old hut only with entertainment and beer. The original 'Dardanelles' was still standing into the 1970s having been used by the Salvation Army for many years.

*Left:* Sunnyside cottages in the 1960s. These 'Old Folks' cottages stood on the site now occupied by Halfords, Argos etc.

# Nelson Colliery

The 'big hill' close by Nelson Village was, in fact, originally two 'big hills' made into one. During the 1970s the bulldozers moved onto the site of the derelict colliery and magically moulded probably the only ski-slope shaped pit heap in Northumberland.

Anyone living in Nelson Village, who is of a certain age, will remember what a marvellous playground the derelict colliery buildings made. Climbing, playing 'tiggy on high', hide and seek and of course, the immense satisfaction in hearing glass breaking as a well aimed stone found the target. The greatest treat, however, lay grey and towering just east of the main colliery buildings. The smaller of the two pit heaps also happened to have the steepest incline on its south face. Standing perhaps 80 feet high the 'heap' was perfect for the exciting, exhilarating and decidedly dangerous sport of 'pit heap tobogganing', once tried never forgotten.

A metal or cardboard sheet big enough to sit on or, a length of conveyor belt, that lay about all over the yard, was ideal for the purpose as it did not wear out and expose the riders

*There appears to have been some dispute in Nelson Village as to whether there was ever two pit heaps or just the one we see today. I hope that this snapshot of Doreen Coppen with baby son Christopher, taken in the mid 1950s, will settle the controversy.*

rear end to an unforgiving surface. This simple equipment was all that was needed for hours of stomach wrenching, bum scraping, pants wetting fun, oh, it also helped if you were daft enough to do it in the first place. I do confess to a sense of wind rushing exhilaration but this was dulled somewhat by sheer terror. As I whizzed by large rocks and jagged lumps of shale it was difficult not to contemplate the possibility of an after life and who I might meet there when my broken and bloody nine years old corpse arrived at the foot of the heap. All of this juvenile jollity, and much more besides, took place during the early 1960s as the colliery had been closed on the 4th January 1958.

Nelson was a result of a merger between the Cramlington and Seaton Delaval Coal Companies who joined forces in May 1929. The result was the Hartley Mains Collieries Company, who immediately set about looking for new coal reserves.

The company sunk four shafts in the Cramlington area. Nelson was the last of these four with its shaft sunk to 360ft to reach the Plessey seam. Another shaft known as the 'back shaft' was sunk to the 'five quarter' seam but ended up becoming a 'staple' shaft. This was an incarnation of something between a vertical shaft and a drift shaft. It had a particularly steep gradient that could only be negotiated by steps cut into the rock.

At its height Nelson employed about five hundred men from the surrounding area and especially from the nearby village of Nelson, that was created specifically to house colliery workers and their families. My father Bill Godfrey was one of them and he was an electrician. I well remember walking down to the 'pit' and sharing his 'bait' with him in the small canteen. Another Nelson worthy was Ted Nevins who was an 'overman' at the colliery. Ted rose to fame in a quite spectacular and heroic manner.

*Underground at Nelson Colliery.*

While two men were working 'in-bye' they discovered a live mortar bomb at the bottom of a ventilation shaft. The two men, Joe Twist and Jimmy Hunter both of Nelson Village, reported the find to the deputy, Ted Nevins. He picked up the bomb and calmly walked 'out-bye' with it. Ted reported the find to the manager who reported to Cramlington police who reported to the Army Ordnance Corps who sent a bomb disposal team from Catterick to deal with the little devil. On arrival they detonated the device behind the pit heap. Quite the hero, I think you will agree.

A more detailed version of the events comes from Dennis Green, who was working at the colliery at the time: 'Jimmy Hunter and Bill Twist worked at the Nelson pit, they were what was known as 'datal hands' meaning, they did a lot of odd jobs. While working night shift, the overman sent them to clean out the bottom of the air shaft. People had a habit of throwing rubbish down it and they took a tub to put the rubbish in.

'Halfway through filling the tub Bill Twist discovered the bomb. He thought that it might be a dud but wasn't sure. Both Bill and Jimmy had been in the army and felt that it was a dud but couldn't be certain. They put it on top of the rubbish in the tub ready to take it to the shaft bottom. As they were getting ready to leave, the night shift deputy came in and saw the bomb. He pushed the tub to the main shaft bottom. Next day in the newspapers headlines said, "Hero deputy saves mine" … Jimmy and Bill's comments were unprintable.

'The bomb disposal unit took the bomb behind the heap and blew it up, they said it was full of concrete. The deputy did not know if the bomb was alive or dead so, he must have been a brave man.'

*A newspaper article recalls the unusual incident at Nelson Colliery.*

## He Walked Calmly
## Miners find live bomb down the pit

*Two men working two miles in-bye at the Nelson Colliery Cramlington, yesterday discovered a live mortar bomb at the bottom of an old ventilation shaft. Joe Twist and Jimmy Hunter, both of Nelson Village, reported their strange find to the first shift deputy, Mr Teddy Nevins also of Nelson, a Salvation Army man. Teddy picked up the live bomb and calmly walked out-bye with it. When he reached the surface he took the bomb to the office of the manager. Mr L. Simpson and made his report. The find was reported to Cramlington police and bomb disposal experts from the Army Ordnance Corps, Catterick were called in. They detonated the bomb near the pit heap about 4.30pm.*

*Right: Mr E. Nevins who carried the live bomb found at Nelson Pit.*

When I left school in 1967, there were far more opportunities for employment than previously. Excluding the war years when high industrial output was needed and of course, man power for the armed services, the school leaver in a coal mining area such as Cramlington had little choice. The biggest employer was the colliery, be it Cramlington, Nelson, Shankhouse, Dudley, Seaton Burn or indeed, any community that relied upon the colliery for its existence. A close close second would have probably been the 'store', the local Co-operative Society. These two became, over the years, the main employers and this situation generated a tradition of employment within many families to the extent that it was to become generational. Dennis Green provides us with an illustration of this in his memories of Nelson colliery.

Dennis had worked for farmer Turnbull, a hard seven day week job, before beginning work at Dudley Colliery. His family were against his move into the pits but he felt that it could be no worse than his long hours on the farm. Dennis' grandfather, father and brother all worked in the mines, his father being transferred to Nelson when West Cramlington closed. The family were native to West Cramlington, which had its own proud community spirit and was self contained enough to boast all of the amenities required to sustain a hard working population. Dennis feels, even now, that he is from West Cramlington, not just Cramlington. After the mine closed the small village lay derelict as its occupants were moved out and dispersed, Dennis' family moved to Nelson Village. He transferred to Nelson pit also, a far more convenient arrangement.

The mine was never modernized to any great degree. While other collieries in the area had received modern cutting equipment, coal was still won by hand at Nelson. Others also had a more convenient method of transporting the coal from the face to the shaft bottom.

Here, this was still done by ponies who were harnessed to the tubs to pull them to the shaft bottom. The ponies, of course, needed to be stabled and looked after properly to enable them to do their work. The man charged with this pleasant task was one of the great characters of Cramlington during the 1960s and '70s.

Joe Dickson was the 'horse keeper' at Nelson for many years and it was his pleasure to keep the stables clean, whitewashed and well ventilated. Having a great love for his ponies Joe kept them well fed and well groomed and would become angry if any were mistreated. This would happen quite often so, when that 'putter' returned next time Joe would make life difficult for him by allocating the most vicious pony in the stable. Dennis Green remembers a pony called 'Dimer': 'One night I was told to take a pony in with me so I told Joe. He said to take the black one and told me his name. I put the halter on him and he would not move. Joe said to give him a polo (mint) or I would be there all night waiting. Why I took the pony, I don't know for there was nothing for it to do when we got underground so, I tied him to a prop and went off to do something else. When I got back 'Dimer' had eaten all the men's sandwiches, except mine! If anyone tried to put the shafts on him his eyes would roll and he would kick and bite. If I did so 'Dimer' was no bother.'

Joe Dickson, known to everyone as 'Joby', was a familiar sight in Cramlington and further afield. He and his horse and cart were in great demand by householders who required something moving, whether it be a garden shed, greenhouse, piano or even the contents of a whole house. When I was five years old we moved from 13 Burdon Avenue to 22 Scott Avenue and it was Joby and Cecil, his long time helper, who did the honours. All I remember of that day was feeling rather grand, sitting on a chair atop of a huge pile of furniture that was roped to the cart. We made slow but steady progress to our new home to the accompaniment of the rhythmic clip, clop and the grating of the metal tyres on the road.

*Joe Dickson, who was horsekeeper at Nelson Colliery for many years, is seen cutting grass at the 'Slack' Klondyke in the mid 1970s. Joe used the resultant hay as feed for 'Jackie', his horse. The wooden building is the Hardware Shop belonging to Eva James.*

*Joe, his horse and cart were also in great demand as furniture movers or any job that required transport. None more so than the time when Joe did a small removal job for the Catholic father of Annitsford. The father mentioned this to his congregation during a service and Joe's popularity as 'Mr Shifter' rocketed. His beautifully turned out horse and cart were also to be seen in many a parade and children's gala.*

Dennis Green's first shift at Nelson was a late shift or, what was known as, the 'old man's shift'. This shift would clear the stones from the face in preparation for the fore shift, who moved coal from the face. He remembers that he 'felt like a leper', as the other miners ignored him. The reason for this – he did not drink at the Nelson Club.

Some of the reasons why Nelson was considered to be a bit of a 'backward' mine are highlighted by Dennis. He found the headlamps cumbersome and heavy, the cage was like 'stepping into a biscuit tin', pumps for clearing water from the workings were not working properly, some of the girders supporting the roof 'were bent like twisted straw' and the conveyor belt that took coal from the face to the loader head was frayed, so that sharp wire protruded from it.

Nelson was heavily censured by the Mines' Inspectorate some years earlier for allowing the underground roadways to deteriorate and as a result the colliery manager was fined. Until the day of its closure in 1958, the mine retained its reputation and Dennis Green, at least, was pleased to say goodbye.

*Above:* Nelson Pit head gear and winder house in the 1950s. The winder man's task was to raise the full tubs, lower the empties and also to lower and raise the miners.

*Right*: Bob Bolton – Winderman. Bob was the founder of Nelson Working Men's Club and was also the scourge of the local bookmakers who finally limited his bets due to a very successful betting system he developed.

*Above:* This is Ralph Spry who practically lived in his shed behind him. A good gardener and a good talker from Nelson Village.

*Left:* Mr Nevins, in his Salvation Army uniform, and his sons Allan and Colin outside the 'Hut' at High Pit.

*Right:* Jack Armstrong in the 1950s. Jack was a Nelson miner who lived in the miners' cottages at Cramlington Station. He could remember a time when life underground was a lot harder and quite a measure more dangerous. Jacks garb is typical of old miners from this period. A collarless two button shirt, suit trousers and waistcoat with a pocket watch, chain and albert, which was sometimes a shield shaped piece of initial inscribed gold or a gold or silver coin. A white silk scarf and flat cap would top off the ensemble and the whole would be supported by a pair of tough leather boots, polished to perfection. Jack spent his last years in his cottage with his two alcoholic friends.

# Childhood Memories

Adam Hamilton of Shankhouse gained this award in 1912, for presumably speaking on a lecture at which he was present. This would have taken place in the Methodist Chapel at Shankhouse and, no doubt, his audience would have been substantial for by 1897 the membership of the 'Band of Hope Union' was in excess of three million. Essentially a temperance movement and therefore part of the great Victorian movement for social reform, the primary target for the 'Band' was children. Various acts of parliament during the late nineteenth century and early twentieth, sought to improve the lot of children. One such was the intoxicating liquors sale to children act of 1901. This prevented the sale of alcohol to children under the age of 14 years but it could still be bought in a sealed or corked bottle. A further act eight years later banned children from entering licensed premises, where before they would have accompanied their parents. The 'Band' became quite influential in the politics of the day being at the forefront in urging the passing of the acts designed to protect children. The 'Band' remains active but has

managed to adapt to the societal changes seen over the years. While the target group remains young people, the focus is now on education around drugs, training educators, and providing drug education to voluntary church and youth organisations.

A class of Cramlington School, circa 1912, unusually with a photograph of this age most of the subjects are named.

Included in the back row are: G. Davison, Hamilton, Stevenson, Willie Bowers. Second row: R. Dickinson, B. Wilson, J. Varty, B. Hardy, B. Draper. Third row: M. Holland, V. Endean, A Pope, Muckle, R. Stephenson, Hamilton. Fourth row: W. Russell, Richmond, E. Hinde, J. Davison, A. Endean. Mr F. Hardy is the master.

Cramlington School, circa 1915. The haystacks in West Farm yard can be seen in the background.

A class group from Cramlington Parkside in the 1920s. The girls appear to be quite outnumbered by the boys and the little girl looks to be half the age of her classmates.

*Above*: Mrs Morgan's class, Cramlington County Secondary School, in 1964. Back row: J. Anderson, B. Jackson, J. Foster, C. Atkinson, J. Snowdon, D. Heads, D. Hampton, K. Bell, M. Carrick. Front row: V. Taylor, E. Simm, A. Wardle, Mrs Morgan, N. Wardle, A. Cherry and B. Bailey. Unfortunately, only one name is unknown.

*Left*: East Cramlington School and Chapel in 1998.

The school yard at Shankhouse, around 1950. Pupils appear to be involved in some sort of country dance. The building beyond the wall is the Methodist Chapel. It was here that 'Saint Andrew of Blyth', Mr Andrew Colvin, became a popular visiting preacher. He was born at Hodgson Hill, Cowpen Square, Blyth in 1811. He became a hewer after spending many years, due to his diminutive size, as a trapper boy. Being brought up in the Methodist faith, Mr Colvin would devote his life to preaching Methodism to the miners of Blyth, Bedlington, Cramlington, Hartley and Shankhouse. It was here that he preached to an unruly congregation of Cornish miners. They had been brought in by the mine owners to work while the Shankhouse men were on strike. The common practice was to evict striking miners and their families from their homes to house 'Blackleg' workers. Mr Colvin reputation as an earnest, effective and ardent preacher was confirmed and enhanced by not only winning over the Cornish men but also converting quite a few in the process. Methodism was established at Shankhouse by Andrew Colvin who preached the first sermon. A master mason called Forster lent his house for the occasion and twenty members of the congregation heard the first sermon. A little later a school room was provided by the use of four colliery houses 'knocked into one'. Membership steadily increased and eventually a chapel was raised seating a congregation of 150 people.

*Right*: Shankhouse School in the mid 1970s. At this time it was no longer a school as the old community had been much reduced by redevelopment. The building became a community resource called 'The Shankhouse' but was demolished soon after this photograph was taken.

# Memories of Christmas in the 1940s by Dennis Green

On Christmas Day, when we were told we could get up, we children rushed downstairs into the kitchen. The presents were in two separate heaps, and hanging from the mantle shelf were our stockings where inside there would be an apple, an orange, nuts, a box of dates and some small presents. We used to get one main present. The last Christmas I remember, I got a garage and four cars, the Beano book, a selection box and a smoker's outfit that consisted of a box of matches, a cigar and a little wooden pipe – all the rest were made of chocolate!

By this time our parents had come downstairs and the first words they said were 'Divvint eat any more chocolate or yill not eat yor brickfist.' Christmas was a family day. We stayed in all day and at midday the men went down the local pub and returned at one o'clock. Then we had our Christmas dinner.

The presents we got in those days were looked after. A fort I got when I was about 10, I gave years later to my grandson. The garage I had for years until my grandfather sat on it, but I still had the cars for a long time afterwards.

On Christmas Eve we used to dress up in old clothes and blacken our faces (in some cases it did not take much doing) and we would go round the houses – this was called 'guysing'. We would sing a Christmas carol, then knock on the door and shout: 'A penny for guysers.' Some times we would be invited in to sing a few songs. When we were invited in we would shove a small boy in front and we would tell him: 'Wipe yar nose and divvint taalk.' At one house we sang about ten carols and all we got was a biscuit. The small boy ate it before we could grab it. Most of the houses we went to were very kind but the odd one would shout: 'Buggar off or aal set thi dog on yi.'

On Boxing day we went out to see what my mates had got from Santy. Jackie Brown used to

*Dennis Green became a judo instructor and here he takes a class in Nelson Village Welfare Hall in the 1960s.*

get something to do with building things as did Bill Rutherford – later on in life they were fitters in factories. Jack Dawson and myself got presents that had no bearing on our future life. Once we had the bright idea of why not buy the small boy a present – as we felt very Christmasy. Someone said: 'Wii cud buy a box of hankies.' Then we had another good idea – buy him a big bar of chocolate as we used to pinch his. Then we did, but someone pointed out it might make his teeth rot, so we decided to eat the chocolate in the interests of his health.

After Boxing Day, New Year's Day was the next event. This was the grown ups' day. We were allowed to sit up till the New Year came in when the first footers arrived smelling of beer. It was a good time to cadge some money off anybody who would be drunk enough. Next day they would say: "Aa thowt aa had more money in me pocket!' New Year's Day was an excuse for the men to get drunk again and it was an excuse for us to get all the loose change they dropped. My mother used to say: 'It will dee yill mair gud in yor pocket than in thi box eggs.' My mother was a very wise woman.

After the holidays, when we went back to school, the school seemed to have lost all the magic of Christmas but we had the Easter holidays to look forward to. On Good Friday it was paste egg day. My mother used to dye hard boiled eggs and it was a tradition to roll them down a hill. The only hill we had was the pit heap but this did not seem like a good idea so we borrowed one from the small boy and rolled it down the heap and it broke up into small bits. He did not seemed to mind until we went for eggs and found out he had eaten ours (exit small boy dodging a hail of stones). My one regret was I never knew the small boy's name. We used to shout: 'Come here yii littil buggar' and he answered to it so that was that.

A scout group comprised of pupils of Cramlington County Secondary School. Back row: Mr Burns (Teacher), ? Yarwood, ?, Mr Pyke (Teacher), ?, B. Godfrey, Mr Hart (Teacher). Middle row: E. Henderson, S. Vintis, G. Luke, R. Flynn, M. Venner, ?, ?. Front row, kneeling: N. Capstaff, ?, R. Capstaff, T. Williams, B. Coppen. The photo was taken at Howick in 1963. We travelled to Howick in the back of a coal lorry belonging to Kelly Coal Merchants of

High Pit, Cramlington. All was well and quite an adventure until the weather took a turn for the worse. I remember that to protect us from the cold and rain, Mr Kelly roped a tarpaulin over us until we reached our destination.

The cast of 'Tom Sawyer' at Cramlington Parkside School around 1965. Included in the back row are: D. Raffle, D. Spooner, R. Derrick, J. Birch, L. Tiplady, J. Riseborough, D. Stephens, K. Wilkinson, F. Hamilton, L. Winship. I'm having difficulty identifying the young chap kneeling and the young chap sitting!

The judo kids of Nelson Village proudly display their trophies.

Some snapshots of Cramlington childhood – from Coronation Day and a football team to dressing up and looking after small animals

Margaret and Kenneth Lawson in Alston Avenue, East Cramlington on Coronation Day in 1953. Behind them is a window display of the new Queen Elizabeth II who has gone on to celebrate her Diamond Jubilee in 2013 and her 90th birthday in 2016.

Margaret and Kenneth Lawson. The nurses outfit was made by Margaret's mother, Kenneth sports a fine cowboy outfit that looks far to good to be homemade (no offence). In the 1950s, Cowboys 'n' Indians was the game of choice for young lads. The Cisco Kid, the Lone Ranger, Roy Rodgers, Hopalong Cassidy etc, all fired the imagination and got kids, like me, roaming the streets and fields, lone star cap gun in hand, searching for 'Pesky Injuns' to battle. If a young fellow possessed such a suit like Kenneth's back then, he would be entitled to feel he was 'King of the wild frontier'.

Shankhouse Juniors football team, 1918.

*Right*: Marjorie and Kathleen White in the back garden of 11 Nelson Avenue with a baby owl. The little chap was orphaned after its mother was shot. She had been doing what all good mothers do simply protecting her offspring. Miners who walked and cycled for the 'First shift' at Nelson Pit, were seen as a threat by Mrs Owl as they passed close to the nest site in the 'pit woods'. She began attacking the 'intruders', scaring most but actually knocking a couple off their bikes. The little fellow in the photo was taken into care and actually became quite tame.

After receiving a copy of 'Cramlington Parkside School Remembered', John Stephens was kind enough to contact me with memories of his time at the school. John is now retired and living in Gloucestershire and still has fond regard for his years at Cramlington. Judging by the items of school memorabilia he kindly sent me John appears to have been much involved in school life and obviously thrived within the educational and social environment. As well as making regular appearances in school musical productions such as 'The Mikado' and 'The Gondoliers' he was awarded the 1947 form prize, the 1948 science prize and the 1949 governors' prize, being made head boy in the same year.

If this wasn't enough to keep him out of strife he also played football for the school team and represented the school in the South Northumberland football team and the South Northumberland schools athletics tournament. After winning the 100 yards' sprint, John went on to represent Northumberland at the 19th Inter County Championships at Carshalton in 1949. John appears to have been the kind of pupil of which every teacher dreams.

Cramlington Secondary Modern School football team, 1947-48. Back row: Mr W.F. Legg, Reggie Holmes, Billy Coulthard, Norman Coates (captain), Malcolm Tucker, ?, ?, ?. Front row: Michael Shanks, John Stephens, Billy Baker, Bill Carruthers, ?.

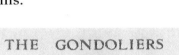

THE GONDOLIERS

Act I

Venice

Act II

Pavilion in the Palace at Barataria
(An interval of three months is supposed to elapse between Acts I and II).

Dramatis Personae

The Duke of Plaza-Toro
(a Grandee of Spain)            REGINALD HOLMES
Luiz (his Attendant)            JAMES HUNTER
Don Alhambra del Bolero
(the Grand Inquisitor)          JOHN STEPHENS
Marco Palmieri                  COLIN WATSON
Giuseppe Palmieri               JOSEPH ARMSTRONG
Antonio    Venetian Gondoliers  JOSEPH WHITE
Francesco                       RONALD MINNS
Giorgio                         COLIN MARK
Annibale                        LESLIE GIBSON
The Duchess of Plaza-Toro       LUCY HEPPLE
Casilda (her daughter)          BETTY HYDE
Gianetta                        MAMIE JOISCE
Tessa                           NELL BARRACLOUGH
Fiametta    Contadine           JUNE NICHOLSON
Vittoria                        JUNE TETLEY
Giulia                          JEAN SYMONS
Inez (the King's Foster-Mother) DOREEN DIX

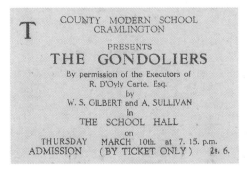

COUNTY MODERN SCHOOL
CRAMLINGTON

PRESENTS

THE GONDOLIERS

By permission of the Executors of
R. D'Oyly Carte. Esq.
by
W. S. GILBERT and A. SULLIVAN
in
THE SCHOOL HALL
on
THURSDAY MARCH 10th. at 7. 15. p.m.
ADMISSION    (BY TICKET ONLY)    2s. 6.

Cast members of 'The Gondoliers', performed in the Hall at Cramlington Modern School on 10th March 1949. Back row: John Stephens, on his own in the big black hat. Front row: James Hunter, Betty Hyde, Lucy Hepple, Reginald (Reggie) Holmes.

*Top left:* The cast list from 'The Gondoliers' Programme.

*Left:* One of the tickets for 'The Gondoliers' printed by the school.

# Bell Ringers

*Left:* Some familiar Cramlington names are represented in this early 20th century photograph of the gentlemen bell ringers of St Nicholas Church. Back row: Mr Warne, Mr R. Swinton, Mr J. Hindmarsh, Mr Simm, Mr W.H. Endean, Mr W. Hume. Front row: unknown, Mr Varty, Mr Endean.

Mr Simm is featured in the photograph below.

*Right:* This well posed photograph dates from around 1900 and shows a precariously seated Arthur Simm and proud dad Oswald. Oswald Simm was born in 1869 and was a bell ringer at St Nicholas Church for almost fifty years. From 1896 until he retired in 1937, Oswald held the proud and glorious title of 'Captain of the Bellfry'. He died in 1948 and, on his tombstone, the bells he played so adroitly are carved. Oswald's wife Ina, died in April 1950. The Simms family lived in South View Place.

Another member of the St Nicholas bell ringers was Mr W.H. Endean, who was a keen footballer and is seen below with the Northumberland Senior Challenge Cup, won while playing for Shankhouse Black Watch. The team won the cup in 1887 and 1891.

Another Shankhouse team with the Northumberland Senior Challenge Cup. Back row: H. Clarkson (Trainer), R. Fletcher (Financial Secretary), R. Simm (Treasurer), R. Robson (Captain), R. Ord, A. Patten, J. Hudson (Secretary). Middle row: W.H. Endean, J. Hamilton, Jos. Briggs, C. Ritson, W.H. Carr (Hon Secretary). Front row: T. Willis, T. Milburn, T. Hume, W. Hedley, M. Gibson. Shankhouse teams won the Northumberland Senior Challenge Cup six times in the 19th century with a hat-trick of wins in 1893, '94 and '95 and an earlier victory in 1886.

Below is an Evening World article describing an unusual bell ringing event at West Cramlington No. 2 (Wrightson) Pit on Saturday, 21st June 1930.

# Coal Seam Christened with Bells

### Newcastle Men's unique peal in mine. First time in history.

Five members of Newcastle Cathedral Guild of Change Ringers have created a world campanological record – that of having rung a successful peal on 10 handbells down a coal mine. They are Messrs W.H. Barber (Conductor), John Anderson, W.J. Davidson, R.S Anderson and A. Deas.

It is the first time in the long history of bell ringing that this has been done. 'Touches' have been rung previously in a coal mine never a full peal. This noteworthy record was accomplished at No 2 Pit, Cramlington when a peal of Grandsire caters comprising 5,003 changes was completed in 2 hours 44 minutes. The peal was also in the nature of a christening for the seam in which it was rung is new and not yet worked. That the peal was to be attempted was a well guarded secret, and only a few personal friends of the ringers including an 'Evening World' representative knew. Secrecy was essential to prevent other centres 'scotching' the attempt and getting in first.

### 50,000 Notes

Collectively, the bells were struck 50,030 times. One stroke missed would have meant failure – the peal would have been uncompleted. Occasionally there was a wavering hand-the conductor would bark an order, then the air was free again. Indeed, success was chiefly due to the efficient conductorship of Mr W.H. Barber, one of the leading bellringers in the country. The peal was rung in an electrically lighted pump room, a short distance from the shaft. Stools were provided, and the air was cool and clean. But an unforeseen incident nearly caused disaster. Unwittingly, the party had left their pit lamps on the roadside. When the peal had progressed seventy five minutes the electric light failed the first time since its installation in the new seam. Without lights the peal would have had to stop for the ringers had to see each other's bells so that they could strike in proper sentence. Cool heads saved the situation.

The referee (Mr J.E.R Keen) and two other's who were listening at the time, rushed for the pit lamps and hurriedly placed them around the ringers. A few seconds and the crisis was over. During those few seconds the ringers were able to carry on. The company's electrician was hurriedly sent for, and after 45 minutes ringing in the light of the pit lamps, electric light was restored. Forty-four minutes later the peal was brought to a triumphant conclusion.

*Right:* The bell ringers who christened the coal seam at West Cramlington No. 2 (Wrightson) Pit in 1930. Back row: Robert S. Anderson (7-8), William J. Davidson (5-6). Front row: Oswald Simm (Referee), Mr T.T. Minns (Colliery Manager), William H. Barber (3-4), Conductor John Anderson (1-2), Adam Deas (9-10), Joseph E.R. Keen (Referee), Durham and Newcastle Association of Change Ringers.

# Joe Leighton of Nelson Village
# A True Geordie Hero

On the night of 8th/9th April 1940, an erstwhile neutral and completely unprepared Norway was invaded by German forces. Amid the chaos a German task force sailed into the Oslofjord with troops intent upon capturing Norway's government and royal family. The guns of the Oscarsberg Fortress had other ideas as the German flagship *Blucher* was sunk and most of the rest of the task force sunk or badly damaged. This incident delayed the German invasion and eventually allowed time for King Haakon VII to escape with his family.

Confusion reigned during the first 24 hours of the invasion and it was during this time that Norwegian forces lost their best equipment. As the defenders rallied and resistance stiffened, German plans were further delayed but this was only a temporary setback. Superior German training, equipment and reinforcements quickly turned defence into a tactical retreat for Norwegian forces.

Support for Norway arrived in the form of elements of the French and British armies, including a detachment of the 1st Battalion Green Howards, based in Richmond, Yorkshire. Amongst the detachment from Richmond was Pte 4392568 J. Leighton, who was completely unaware that he was about to embark upon a true, life defining adventure that is scarce believable, even in these days of 'tall tales'.

The Allied forces that landed at Narvik and other points on the Norwegian coast had initial success in stemming the German advance. At this time however, the situation in Europe was deteriorating and the British government decided to evacuate its forces from Norway. Not all of the British force managed to get out however and Joe and some companions watched from the mountains as the king, his family and what remained of the Norwegian government were evacuated aboard the cruiser HMS *Glasgow*. Joe always said that the British government had more interest in saving the Norwegian gold reserves from the Germans than any king or government!

Joseph Leighton was born on Christmas Day 1918, and spent his early years living with his grandparents at Seaton Burn. His grandfather Roscoe was a miner at Seaton Burn Colliery and Joe remembered him telling stories about the Great War. Grandfather Roscoe had responded to the call for experienced miners to join up as Tunnelling Regiments were being formed. As a member of 172 Company Royal Engineers, granddad Roscoe and his chums, would tunnel under German positions, on the Western Front, lay huge charges of high explosives and then get out, very quickly. He had made his own identification bracelet out of brass, just in case.

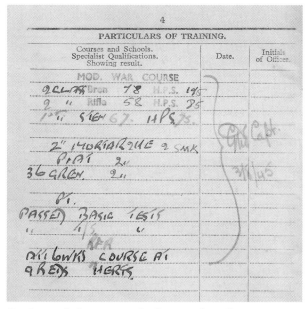

*Joe's training record shows that he was proficient in all of the standard issue infantry weapons of the time. A dangerous little chap, our Joe!*

Joe appears to have lived with a number of family members during his early years. As well as his grandparents, an aunt and his own parents are remembered by the family. He must at one time have lived at West Cramlington for he distinctly remembered being sent to George Clough's brewery by his father to have him fill his can with ale.

Joe, like most young men of the area and era, was probably expecting to work out his days at one of the local collieries. The traditions of the coalfield were many, one of which being the custom of son following father into the mines. In many cases this was less like a custom and more of a necessity as employment opportunities were particularly scarce. The annals of the industry record many accidents, disasters and deaths. The roll of casualties often record the names of fathers and sons and other close relatives lost to their families through flooding, rock falls, explosions and a hundred other ways of being maimed or killed. After starting work at Seaton Burn Colliery, Joe's course veered off into something completely different but inherently more dangerous.

It is not clear why he chose the Green Howards but Joe enlisted on the 15th November 1939. His 'Trade on Enlistment' is shown to be that of 'rope lad', which may put him as working in one of the local collieries until this date. After a period of training Joe and his comrades, as we have seen, were sent to Norway to help in the defence and to evacuate the Norwegian royal family and government. Joe had sustained a leg wound, which was not particularly serious but enough to slow him down while trying to escape from German troops. Placed aboard a ship along with other captured British troops, Joe and his companions were first taken to Oslo and from there to a POW camp in Poland.

Stalag XXA, was located in northern Poland at a place called Torun, situated on a tributary of the River Vistula. This ancient town was surrounded by a complex of defensive forts and it was these forts that were used to house POWs. Captured soldiers from France, Italy, Norway, Poland and Russia were sent to Torun and it was here that the 403 British soldiers captured in Norway were brought in June of 1940, among them was Joe Leighton.

Joe's first attempt at escape failed as he was quickly recaptured by the German police. He was forced to live on bread and water for a while but still planned on making another bid to escape. He had told the Germans that he was a farmer so that he would be able to work outside, with more opportunities to escape. At this time the prisoners were often 'loaned out' to local industries and state farms as free labour. As a private Joe was required to work in one of the labour units, sergeants and above, in rank, were not required to work as articled in the Geneva Convention. In January 1944, during one of the coldest winters on record, Joe and three others finally managed to escape; they headed east.

This postcard, bearing official German identification stamps on the back, was sent home by Joe in August 1942. He is seen in the centre, flanked by happy, healthy looking comrades.

| Ther | March 8 | Wea |
|------|---------|-----|
| TODAY RECIEVED FIVE POUNDS FIRST IN FIVE YEARS SENT AIR MAIL LETTER HOME FROM TURKEY | | |
| Ther | March 9 | Wea |
| RECIEVED A GIFT OF SHAVEING KIT FROM RED CROSS 100 cigs | | |

A small pocket diary issued by the Germans to their captives. As well as some names and addresses of some of his companions and some football scores taken from an old English newspaper Joe records, in March 1942, '... received a gift of shaving kit from Red Cross ... 100 cigs'. It is a shame that he did not record more.

At some point, fairly soon after escaping probably, they are picked up by Polish resistance fighters, no doubt questioned to make sure that they were not German and Joe, at least, decided to stay with them.

Joe had a tattoo on his right forearm that, according to his son Brian – 'didn't look like anything in particular.' He described a strange patter of intertwined circles looking for all the world like it was a work in progress, unfinished. He remembers Joe, on one of the rare occasions he actually spoke of his war experiences, saying that the tattoo was placed there by the Poles. It was a symbol that they understood and was a mark of identification, without it you could not be trusted. It was during this time that Joe had a most harrowing experience, one that was to haunt him for many years.

In this area of Poland, as well as camps for POWs there were also the infamous concentration camps such as, Majdanek, Treblinka, Chelmno, Sobibor, Belsen and Auschwitz-Birkenau. With Russian forces driving into Poland from the east the people who operated these, what were later discovered to be 'extermination camps', thought it best that they did not allow themselves to be captured and have to explain why they had murdered millions of Jews, Gypsies, Slavs or anyone else that contravened the Aryan ideal. Many of these places were simply abandoned and the surviving inmates left to fend for themselves.

While out with a group of fighters one day Joe witnessed 'dead people walking'. From the woods staggered scores of 'human skeletons' with hollow eyes and skin stretched tight over fleshless bones. They had been hiding in the woods in fear of the camp guards returning but came out on seeing friendly forces. Some of the fighters went off and returned leading a cow, which was shot, butchered and boiled, along with some vegetables, into a broth for the inmates. This must have seemed like a Godsend to people whose faith must have been shaken by their experiences.

The Polish government presented Joe with a medal in 1990, the Bronze Medal For Bravery on the Battlefield. It was a time that he found himself in a Polish village with resistance fighters, which came under attack by German troops. The Germans were elite SS soldiers and their attack was successfully fought off by Joe and his companions. At 70

*Joe's medals – the Polish award is at the left.*

years distance it is now impossible to say what personal acts of bravery Joe performed to earn his award. The name of the village in Poland also cannot be determined. The whole story is like an old film with missing frames, jumping from one scene to another and with no means of understanding how we arrived at where we are. Like many veterans Joe was reluctant to talk about his experiences during the war. When he did begin to speak however, a certain point in the story was reached, his voice would falter, out came his hanky and a tearful silence followed.

Consequently, Joe's family knew little of his exploits. They knew that he had been a prisoner, knew he had been awarded a medal but he gave them very little else. Brian Leighton remembers watching films or documentaries on TV with his father when Joe was an old man. Joe would often say that he had fired one of those guns or driven one of those vehicles or had been inside a tank. Brian didn't think much of it at the time but confirmation and a further tantalizing glimpse into Joe's past was to come from an unlikely source.

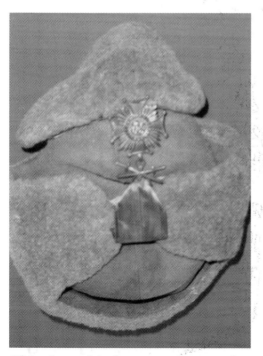

*This sheepskin hat was given to Joe by a Russian captain. The winter of 1944 was one of the severest on record and German troops suffered particularly badly through lack of appropriate winter clothing.*

Brian took his father to a medical appointment at Wansbeck Hospital, Ashington. Brian waited while Joe was lead into a room by a nurse. After a while Joe returned accompanied by the nurse. The nurse paid great attention to Joe, saying that he was a hero. Brian did not fully understand what had happened and, as it turned out, missed an opportunity to fit more pieces of the puzzle together. Joe's nurse happened to be Polish and from the very village that was successfully defended by Joe and the resistance fighters during the winter of 1944. Her accent had obviously been recognized by Joe and a conversation followed that touched upon his experiences in Poland during the war. By this time his memory had faded and he was increasingly confused. Brian tried to contact the Polish nurse but found that she no longer worked at Wansbeck Hospital. The name of the village in Poland remains undetermined but the events of that day seem to have been preserved in the oral traditions of its inhabitants.

As Russian forces advanced through Poland they came into contact with various elements of the Polish resistance force, with Joe still among them. It was here that an unlikely relationship was to develop.

A Russian captain who 'spoke to us in perfect English' recognized Joe's northern accent. The captain had studied medicine at Kings College in Newcastle for five years before the war and must have immediately recognized Joe's Geordie 'twang'.

It is not certain how their relationship developed but having heard of the action in the village, from some captured German soldiers, the captain must have thought that his new allies were able and brave fighters.

A friendship formed under such desperately dangerous circumstances must create a bond that would outlast all others. Joe stayed with the Russian captain and his command as they advanced through Poland, with Berlin as the final objective. Not only had Joe been inside a tank, he had actually operated the hull machine gun in a huge T34! In 1970 Joe travelled to Russian in an effort to find the captain. Unfortunately, Joe learned that, only a few months after their last meeting in the winter of 1944, the captain had died in the spring of the next year during the battle for Berlin.

We next find Joe at Odessa, on the Black Sea, awaiting repatriation to England. A newspaper report of the time states that he had been a POW for five years and was freed by Russian forces. Joe was never debriefed on return so no record of his exploits, after being captured in Norway, exist in the regimental archives of the Green Howards. Joe, like many of his breed did not want to talk about what he had experienced, even on an official level. He was reluctant to relive what must have been very painful incidents in his past for the rest of his life. Only occasionally would he allow a glimpse into a past that none of us can imagine and this was done in a manner befitting, self effacing, humble and without the need to glamourize his actions. Joe's story could have been lifted straight from the pages of 'Commando Comic', the difference of course being, that this one is true.

Joe was 'demobbed' and returned to Nelson Village and a, slightly less dangerous, job at Nelson Pit before becoming a driver for the NCB. He retired while in his early 60s spending a great deal of his time allotment gardening but still retained a connection to his past life through membership of the British Legion, the Green Howards Association and the POW's Association. In 1990, the Polish government presented him with the Bronze Cross of Merit, 'For services rendered on the battlefield', in recognition of his part in defending the village against German troops. Joe was particularly proud of this award and his family continue to be so. Joe died in September 2010.

*Joe is seated at the left, next to Joe Moore, at Nelson Village in 1994 on the 50th anniversary celebrations of the D-Day landings. The younger people in those image would have little idea of what it was all about other than a bit of a treat, with pop and cakes later.*

*Another postcard sent from the German POW Camp, Stalag XXA. Joe is centre back row.*

# The 'Hostel Estate'

The photograph on the right shows my grandmother 'Sissy' Collier and dog Mick, in the back garden of 36, Village Road, in the 1950s. This little photograph is interesting because, in the background is seen one of the original buildings on the site now occupied by the 'Hostel Estate'.

During the early years of the Second World War, as the bombing by the Luftwaffe of major British cities and industrial centres intensified, large sections of the civilian population of cities like London, Liverpool and Manchester were evacuated to areas of the country that were considered to be safe from aerial attack. September of 1939, saw the beginning of Operation Pied Piper, which was to relocate more than three million people from urban areas within officially classified 'evacuation' zones. These were to include children and mothers, old and disabled and pregnant women. Cramlington was within the zone designated 'reception' so in 1939-40 the camp on Village Road was built under the Government sponsored 'Camps Act'.

Designed by architect T.S. Tait, this would be one of thirty such camps built in various rural locations around the country. The buildings were single story bungalows, perhaps 40ft long and 20ft wide and roofed with corrugated asbestos sheets (horror!). They were, quite simply, barracks with no interior comforts other than, what can only be described as, stalls. Six or eight stalls occupied each side of the building, the centre being open for its length, rather like stables and furnished with bunk beds and a wardrobe but little else. Whole families were to occupy these cramped, virtually public spaces but only for the purpose of sleeping as the site also boasted a wash block, dining hall and kitchens and a recreation hall. There was also a medical facility in the form of a clinic that assessed children on arrival and visiting local doctors attended to medical needs.

The 'Camp', as it became known, was intended only as a temporary measure, a transit camp for evacuated families who would find more permanent placements elsewhere. Private house owners were 'expected' to take in evacuated children and families if they had spare rooms in their properties.

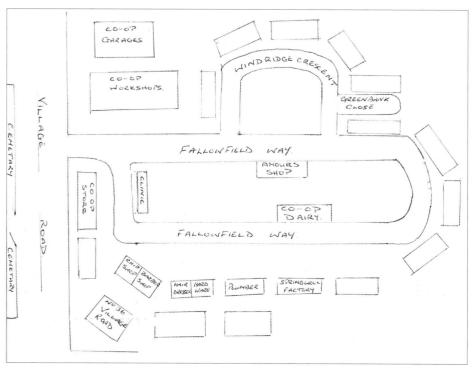

*Left:* This map is necessarily incomplete and maybe inaccurate as it was kindly drawn from memory by Malcolm Gibson of Nelson Village, who delivered milk to the estate many years ago. If anyone can add to or correct errors in the map I would be grateful. Also, if any former residents of the 'camp' have memories and photographs they would like to share, again this would be welcome. The present Hostel Estate occupies roughly the same area as the wartime buildings.

So the 'camp' saw a continual turnover in occupants, some staying a few days or a few weeks at worst until mass evacuations were deemed impractical as the aerial threat diminished. As the last of the evacuees left, local Civil Defence personnel took over the site.

The facilities in the camp were retained in order to house and feed the various service people and volunteers who did duty there. The stable-like sleeping quarters would not be up graded until after the war and it is unclear as to the number of buildings that were in use at this time. Units of the Home Guard regularly spent time here, as did ARP and fire and ambulance personnel.

At the end of the war the site and its buildings was returned to the Local Authority by the Government. This had been a stipulation at the outset and with this in mind the layout of the 'camp' had been planned for future use after the original purpose was not required. Instead of regimented rows of buildings the site was planned as a quite pleasant housing estate, with space for gardens and green areas. The bigger buildings, those that had housed kitchens, dining hall, wash block and recreation hall, were demolished and the rest given over to social housing. The 'stalls' were removed and with the addition of partition walls, sitting rooms, bedrooms and very small kitchens and bathrooms, these erstwhile barrack blocks were transformed into something a bit more cosey.

The site gradually took on an air of self sufficiency as some of the buildings were taken over for commercial and industrial use. The clinic still operated well into the 1960s. Cramlington Co-op had a branch there while Mr Lofthouse (later to take over as postmaster at Nelson Village) conjured up particularly fine fish and chips. Fenwick Barrass, who had a black enamelled paraffin stove that smoked incessantly (as did its owner), was a barber for the chaps and Lydia James, of Nelson Village, ran a hairdressing business for the ladies. Also on site was a hardware shop, a light engineering firm, a car repair garage and a baker who made wonderful pies. So all in all, living on the 'Hostel', as it was increasingly called, meant that you could want for little else and with the Burton House only 200 yards away just about every need was catered for.

I believe that it was some time in the late 1960s that it was decided to demolish the old buildings and build a new estate on the site. I particularly remember a 5th November bonfire built entirely of interior doors, and anything else that would burn, taken from the old houses. They had been empty for some time and therefore prey to the natural curiosity of the young.

Today the present estate, constructed within the bounds of the original camp, retains an echo of its past still with the name, Hostel Estate.

The manager and all female staff of the Pickle factory at Nelson Village in the late 1940s / early '50s. After the camp buildings were demolished the Springwell Factory moved to the above premises. The building still survives as workshops.

# Shankhouse

Shankhouse Colliery. 4709

Shankhouse Colliery, around 1920. This image from an old picture postcard does not actually qualify as a snapshot but it is used to 'set the scene' as it were.

Virtually the same view but the colliery is closed and workmen are taking down the headgear in the 1960s.

Two men pose for the camera at Shankhouse Colliery in 1951.

Tubs leaving Shankhouse for a return journey to Nelson Colliery on the endless ropeway.

A patch of sunlight illuminates this group of 'banksmen'. Thomas Rice stands at right.

*Above*: Shankhouse Colliery Office, 1951. Thomas Rice, wearing cap, was colliery blacksmith for many years.

*Left*: A glitter postcard from around 1920. A little corny no doubt but indicative of Shankhouse being big enough and proud enough of itself to advertise the fact.

Newcastle Road, Shankhouse.    4708

*Above*: Newcastle Road, Shankhouse, around 1920. Another cheat as this image is a postcard. The photograph was taken on the same day as colliery postcard on the previous page.

*Right*: In the garden of his home in Shankhouse Terrace, Thomas Rice and his granddaughter, Elizabeth Walker, and friends enjoy a sunny day.

# Doctor William Brown of Shankhouse

The following tribute to Doctor William Brown was written shortly after his death in May 1954, who for 27 years faithfully served the people of Shankhouse as Medical Practitioner. And most ably acted, as their guide, sage and philosopher.

*Right:* Doctor Brown of Shankhouse.

*Below:* Doctor Brown's three daughters, Joyce, Rosemary and Diana, in fancy dress for a show at Hartford Welfare Hall in 1940.

There's a bit of land, a narrow plot
In the old church yard on Horton Hill
To Shankhouse folk 'tis a hallowed spot
There lies their Doctor by God's will.

He's lying there at his last rest
Lord may he rest in peace;
He was a friend, one of the best,
Their praise of him will never cease.

His brisk step up the garden path,
His rat-tat on the door;
His cheerful voice, his happy laugh,
Alas! They'll never hear them more.

He shared their fun, enjoyed their jokes,
He shared their sorrow and their grief
They'll miss him much, the Shankhouse folk
His stay with them was all too brief.

He walked with death but carried on,
With courage and unafraid.
Now to a better life he's gone,
His memory will never fade.

To his wife and daughters in their grief,
Just this I humbly say,
It is my firm and staunch belief,
You'll meet again some future day.

So, 'till that great day comes along,
Dear friends may I say this,
Be brave and like him carry on,
I'm sure would be his foremost wish.

*Anthony Bryden*

Not only did the good doctor work in Shankhouse he also lived in the community, with his wife and three daughters. This was at a time when there were no health centres as we know them today and very often a local GP's surgery was held in his own home. Daily home visits to patients delivering sound medical practice and sage advice, on a range of topics, simply enhanced Dr Brown's standing within the small community of Shankhouse, to almost legendary status. The doctor had been ill for some time but continued to perform his duties in Shankhouse and the wider Cramlington area. On the day he died, 9th May, his last house call was to Mr Carruthers, at Nelson Village.

I have spoken with many people over the years with memories of the good doctor and all agree that he was a kind, considerate, professional who was held in high regard by the good folks of Shankhouse and everyone who knew him.

A memorial to Dr Brown in Nelson Village Welfare Hall.

# Royal Celebrations

Coronation Day – 3rd June 1953. The residents of Nelson Village celebrate the event with a parade. Here, a pipe band, livens up Arcot Avenue while the crowd keeps pace.

Residents in fancy dress are carried on a decorated lorry belonging to Robert Deuchar Ltd. Robert Deuchar's Brewery was based in Sandyford, Newcastle and they were one of the main brewers for the area until 1959, when taken over by Newcastle Breweries.

*Left*: The parade must have made its way to the bowling green or 'Bowla', as we kids used to call the field to the east of the village. It had actually been a bowling green and tennis courts in the days when Nelson was known as 'Cramlington Hostel'. This photo shows 'Good Queen Bess', looking very regal standing between the good luck chimney sweep and Old Mother Riley.

*Right:* Meanwhile the Coronation party is in full swing in the front room of No 36 Village Road. The table is groaning with the weight of the finest cakes on offer at Cramlington 'Store'. The toast to her Majesty was given with liberal amounts of sherry and port and a few games of whist. It was fortunate that most of the ladies present lived locally. Among the monarch's loyal subjects are myself, being held by my grandmother,

Cissie Collier, Mrs Whiteman, Sally Green, Beattie Godfrey, Sybil Baker and Mrs Reid.

*Left*: Another Royal celebration at Nelson Village this time the Silver Jubilee in 1977. This snap shows her Majesty Queen Elizabeth and the Duke of Edinburgh also known as Kathleen Mullen and Andrew Hyde.

'Speedy' Wright and 'Spot' Philips add a little sophistication to the proceedings.

Andrea and Kathleen Mullen – The Queen of Nelson Village.

*Left*: Silver Jubilee celebrations in 1977 outside Nelson Post office – that used to stand at the top of Scott Avenue. Present are: Joan Young, Jean Appleby, Maureen Welford, Mary Austin, Speedy Wright, Bill Phillips, A. Cowl, M. Mullen, M. Dixion, M. McSparran, S. Ridley, C. Fairhurst, Maureen Burdis and Mrs White, who owned the shop, at front

The Jubilee year also saw the visit to Cramlington of the Queen and Prince Philip on 15th July 1977 – attended by an illustrious party, including the Duke of Northumberland. The Royal party arrived at Cramlington Station. It was probably the first time in 50 years that the old station received a lick of paint!

*Right:* Her Royal Highness and Prince Philip leave the station bound for Concordia. I was somewhere in that crowd!

*Right:* The Royal party leaving Cramlington to be guests of the Duke of Northumberland at Alnwick Castle.

*Left:* A momento of the Royal visit to Cramlington in 1977 in the form of the Post Office First Day Cover. An 8p stamp (how cheap was that) has been franked with a crowned lion rampant and the date of the visit.

*Right:* Yet another Royal celebration this time at Alston Avenue East Cramlington, where a street party was held to celebrate the marriage of Prince Charles and Lady Diana Spencer. There's nothing like a hokey cokey to get the party going.

# Cramlington New Town

In January of 1964, the Northern Architectural Association issued a plan for a 'Linear City'. This new 'City' was to stretch from Durham to Cramlington, a distance of almost 30 miles. Having connections to the A1 and other routes, the plan was to regenerate the region's environment over a proposed two mile width. It also proposed to: 'raze obsolete towns as too many towns and villages repelled the visitor.'

The president of the Association, Mr M. Hayton said that: 'the team responsible have studied this subject very thoroughly' … and believed that …. 'they had found an immediate basis for planning.' The plan was to become known as the 'Growth Zone' but its inception was not welcomed by all.

Northumberland County Council criticized the fact that the whole industrial region north of the river Blyth was not to be included in the new zone. This region included Ashington, Bedlington and Newbiggin having a total population of almost 100,000 people. The Council felt that high unemployment in these communities could be alleviated if more favourable economic and industrial conditions were not created elsewhere. Furthermore, it asked for the grants and allowances, that would be inherent within the 'Growth Zone', to be extended to lessen the likelihood of industrial stagnation.

The earlier 'Hailsham Report' proposed that Government assistance be given to: 'that part of the North East region which has the most favourable conditions for self-sustaining growth.' The areas outside of the zone plainly displayed a disincentive to industrial expansion. As traditional industries decline then private and government investment is required to maintain and develop economies and to sustain population. If there is no share in industrial development all of the financial and social penalties are paid by these communities.

Within the 'Zone' provision was also made for the creation of 'New Towns', principally those of Killingworth and Cramlington. In April of 1964, Mr Donald Slater, Assistant

*Test drilling on the site of the Parkside estates in 1975. The Shankhouse council estate is under construction in the background.*

County Planning Officer, attended a public meeting to explain the Council's plans and how things would change for the better in the future. The process had already began as the first phase of the new Wilkinson Sword factory was up and running. Two shifts of workers were quickly employed by the company and other factories on the site north of the railway station were planned. New bus routes, roads and housing were also anticipated so, an air of excitement and expectation pervaded the district.

To meet the anticipated rise in population, from 5,000 to 48,000, house building needed to increase year on year until a set for 1981 was reached. The old village centre was to receive a facelift but would remain essentially the same. Derelict areas, such as the long abandoned village of West Cramlington, would be reborn as park land, playing fields and the colliery spoil heaps remodelled, grassed and wooded. This was also true of Nelson Colliery were the twin heaps were to be transformed into a football ground and stadium. All of these developments and the new housing estates would be linked by pedestrian and cycle paths, plus three new schools all within a five year development plan.

Cramlington was the only new town development in the country to begin with factories before the development of housing. Other such schemes in the past have had problems in social amenities not matching the house building programme. In this case it was felt that any problems could be quickly dealt with as each would be planned to keep pace with the other. However, all was not quite well with this mid 1960s view of a social Utopia. A report prepared by the Planning Committee in May 1964, warned that the development of the new towns of Killingworth and Cramlington on the present basis would prove extremely strenuous on County finances. This would inevitably lead to a rise in the County rate, which in turn would make the area less attractive to investment in new industries which, after all, was the idea of the new towns in the first place.

Originally, the schemes for building the new towns was estimated to cost £40 million and Northumberland Council decided to push ahead on its own. It had become clear that the grants that central Government had promised would not reach the Council's expectations and only a small contribution was received to offset the Council's expenditure. Given the circumstances a complete review of the project was held by the Planning Committee who recommended that the development of Cramlington should continue. The Minister of Housing and Local Government was asked to take over to continue the development of Killingworth and to provide financial assistance to Cramlington. It was felt that, as with other development areas in Durham and elsewhere, the expenditure for new town development should be met by the Government. The Minister, Sir Keith Joseph, agreed to re-examine the situation of finance 'sympathetically', in the light of further information. Despite the prevailing uncertainty, expansion of the first industrial site to the west of Cramlington Station, continued with proposals for a new factory. Subject to negotiations with the Council, Commercial Plastics were to join George Angus and Wilkinson Sword on Cramlington's first Industrial Estate.

During a debate on the two new towns of Killingworth and Cramlington in June 1964, the Parliamentary Secretary to the Ministry of Local Government, Mr F.V. Corfield, announced to the House that the Government would give only limited assistance to the two schemes. Although Northumberland Council had applied for financial aid, existing legislation was to limit the Government's response. The New Towns Act, also placed limitations upon the County Council as to how much it could borrow. Mr Corfield suggested that Northumberland County Council, in the light of its financial difficulties: 'whether the value of the scheme is not sufficiently great to make it worthwhile giving up its own immediate control to a new town corporation.' He felt that this was the

*Cramlington from the railway bridge in 1973. Station Terrace has gone and work is beginning on the new shopping centre.*

only way in which a new town could operate under the Act but was aware of the problems and wanted to help. The Cramlington enterprise was conceived as a joint venture between the County Council, the Local Authority and a consortium of builders.

It was the builders who owned most of the land that had been scheduled for development into housing areas. In July of 1964, Seaton Valley Urban District Council approved the tender by Hawthorn Leslie of Jarrow, to build 152 dwellings in Cramlington. Subject to approval the firm were to erect 20 one bedroom terrace, 40 two bedroom terrace, 48 three bedroom terrace and 44 two bedroom semi-detached dwellings at a cost of £311,965. These houses were not built in the traditional manner but constructed in pre-fabricated sections. The design and construction later proved questionable so, during the 1970s, these dwellings on the Allensgreen Estate, were reinforced with brickwork.

Two of the biggest North East builders at the time were J.T. Bell and William Leech, who concentrated their efforts in house building. The plan was to build 12,000 new houses, rented and private, over various sites in Cramlington. By virtue of an agreement between Seaton Valley Council and Messrs Wm Leech Ltd, workers in the new factories could purchase their homes on easy terms. On payment of a £50 deposit, which was deducted from the purchase price, the Council would then grant a 100% mortgage to the buyer. This was only granted on ability to repay and a third party signing a guarantee bond. Repayments over 30 years were £4 3s per week with interest at one quarter percent above that charged by the Public Loans Board.

The development plan allowed for 1,165 acres to be set aside for residential use, 300 acres for recreation with the town centre covering 60 acres and 530 acres set aside for industrial use. On Friday, 23rd October 1964, the first industrial estate in Cramlington was officially opened by the Duke of Northumberland, Lord Lieutenant of the county. This 180 acre site already held Wilkinson Sword, which was in production and others nearing completion. Development of these sites continued with Bassington and South Nelson housing smaller, more specialized businesses, rather than those like the huge, now defunct, Brentford Nylons site at South Nelson.

Alongside continuing development there is re-development. The site of the first big employer in the Cramlington area, Wilkinson Sword, has been cleared for housing that is nearing completion (November 2016). 2014 saw the demolition of the old school in the village, completely changing the skyline in favour of a housing development.

The origin of the village of Cramlington goes back to Saxon England but the origin of what we have today is barely 50 years old. The title of 'New Town' was added to postal addresses and rail and bus destination boards until well into the 1970s or even '80s. Eventually the shine wore off the place and we were not 'New' anymore. Today, Cramlington encompasses a far larger area and, losing the 'New Town' tag, we are satisfied with the original name.

*This muddy field in 1987 would eventually contain the parking area and the 'out of hall' shopping outlets.*

*Safeway's main entrance inside Manor Walks in the 1990s.*

An advertisement that appeared in the 'Blyth News' in 1963 for John T. Bell Builders.

# Days To Remember

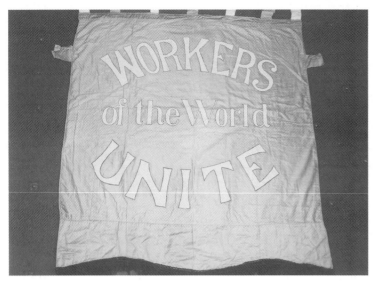

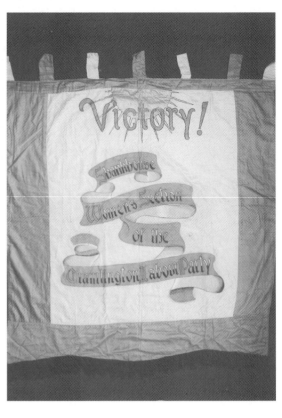

*Above and right:* The front and back of the banner for the Shankhouse Women's Section of the Cramlington Labour Party. The first comment regarding this unique survivor of Cramlington's past is that it was not professionally made. The great colliery lodge banners of the Durham and Northumberland coalfields where made by specialist firms to the specifications of individual collieries. Some of these banners were so big and grand that a crew of sometimes six burly miners was needed to carry them during parades. Our banner is dwarfed by these. Measuring only 3'6" x 3'9", it could be carried by means of a cross and two side poles by two considerably less but in some cases more burly miners' wives. One of these was Mary Anne Hamilton of Shankhouse, who also had a hand in making the banner. The date is uncertain but the feeling is that this symbol of political solidarity was born of the social and political turmoil during the years following the Great War when the 1920s saw upheaval in many countries as new orders fought to establish themselves. The General Strike of 1926, the derailing of the 'Flying Scotsman' at Cramlington and the 'Hunger Marches', especially that of Jarrow, of the 1930s would have spawned the passion and determination that went into this incredible survivor.

Two photos of Robert Taylor in typical 1950s schoolboy dress. The only item that is non regulation is the miner's helmet and cap lamp. Robert, a cousin of Majorie White, now Mullen, is seen standing in Nelson Pit yard with his uncle John White, Majorie's father, who was an 'onsetter' and a quite docile looking pit pony. Robert was on holiday from his home in Epsom and was presented with the helmet as a keepsake. He wore it all the way home to Surrey.

Cramlington Women's Institute liked dressing up. This photograph could show a celebration bash thrown around 1930. Included are ladies as teachers, nurses, gypsies and queens – including Victoria. Unfortunately, the reason for the dressing up is unknown.

They are at it again! More dressing up for Cramlington ladies. The occasion is unknown and are the suffragettes real or part of a pageant? Note the lady on the far left with the hammer with which she would drive home her point.

For many years there have been certain sayings in Cramlington (and no doubt other places) like: 'He should be in Morpeth ...' or 'You'll drive me to Morpeth ...' or '... to be taken to Morpeth.' This had nothing to do with train or bus services (which were always quite frequent). Morpeth was the home of St George's Hospital which housed the 'insane' so 'Morpeth' became a word for 'men in white coats' who would whisk one away never to be seen again at the merest sniff of outlandish behaviour. Our snapshot dates from 1935 when nurse Mary Beatrice Collier, of 36 Village Road, Cramlington is twenty-one years old. She stands before her place of employment, St George's Hospital, Morpeth that looks more like a factory than a place of care and refuge. Mary had to give up her career after being hurt while helping another nurse who was attacked by a patient.

The wedding of Mr Reginald Allan, son of Revd T.P Allan, vicar of St Nicholas, Cramlington to Miss Kathleen Elsie Bodger of Cramlington Hall. Among those present are the bride and groom's parents. The photograph was taken at Cramlington Hall.

*Right*: An honoured guest at the Nelson Village Silver Jubilee celebrations in 1977 was Doctor Meeke, seen here receiving some flowers. Dr Meeke was a much respected practitioner in Cramlington for many years and practised alongside her husband Dr Charles from their surgery at Quarry House.

Speaking of Dr Charles – anyone who remembers him will recall a quiet spoken unhurried, pleasant and knowledgable MD (rather like everyone's favourite granddad!) He was also, shall we say a little unpredictable and a little surprising in some of his eccentricities. If on visiting the Quarry House Surgery you were prepared to wait while Dr Charles showed another patient around his beautiful Quarry garden with his collection of fine roses. Or to be a little shocked when the doc entered the waiting room carrying a large saw, its teeth sheared with red paint in imitation of blood. Or listen to his stories of his childhood in Ireland (he had the most delicious lilt to his voice) and many more 'treatments' not sanctioned by the BMC, then you would generally have a good time, ailments allowing of course!

The entertainment value was high and the medical expertise was of its time, compare all of this to a visit to a surgery today.

The old doc liked people and he really felt that his non-medical treatments helped recovery. This all got out of hand somewhat later on. Late one afternoon while delivering groceries to Quarry House from Harry James shop from who I worked at the time. I chanced upon a strange tableaux. Parking the old Wolseley and taking the groceries to the back door my way was blocked by the paper boy. He stood still holding his paper bag in front of his body in a sort of protective manner. Nothing strange about this I hear you say, only he had balanced on his head and empty baked bean tin. The young lad's face had a look that can only be described as one of sheer terror. For at the other end of the yard stood Doc Charles, in dressing gown and slippers taking careful aim at the tin can with an air rifle! To say that this was a little surprising would be an under statement. Not the sort of thing one encounters on a daily basis. It must have been in the early 1970s after the doc had retired, that this William Tell-ish episode took place. Whether the can was split, like the apple, I cannot tell. The doc acknowledged my arrival and motioned me to put down the groceries by pointing at the rifle to the ground. Whereupon, I made a hasty exit back to the old Wolseley. The paperboy's expression had changed from terror to mute resignation as he awaited the Doc's attentions. As I got in to the car I thought I heard the rattle of a tin can but not thankfully the unmistakable howl of a wounded paperboy!

The doc once sewed up my left knee many years ago. A dab hand at needlework.

Nelson villagers of a certain age will probably recognise this muddy lane as the 'Trot'. This is the track of the rail line where coal was transported by an endless ropeway to the screens at Shankhouse Colliery. This particular section is now the cycle path that runs by the houses and shops at Brockwell.

The Methodist Chapel at Hartford Colliery shortly before its removal in 1975. Clad in corrugated metal sheets the chapel was locally known as the 'Tin Church'.

*Right*: A flooded underpass after heavy rain in 1975. Things have not changed much after 40 years as this underpass, lying directly behind the Marks and Spencers outlet, is still plagued by flooding.

*Right*: The same underpass in 2016 – Nothing changes very much!

Two photos of the Cramlington Gala in 1981.

*Above*: Gala Saturday has attracted quite a crowd to the 'shows' entertainment and sports – a traditional mix for galas. Is it me or, does everyone seem to be heading for the beer tent! The houses in the background are those of Sunnyside and work continues on the new shopping centre at right. Asda now covers most of the area.

*Left*: All the fun of the fair! The new police station is top right.